ROMANIA

GOSPEL AND CULTURES PAMPHLET 3

ROMANIA
Orthodox Identity at a Crossroads of Europe

Ion Bria

WCC Publications, Geneva

Cover design: Edwin Hassink
Cover photo: The outside walls of a painted church in
Moldavia (WCC/Peter Williams)

ISBN 2-8254-1175-2

© 1995 WCC Publications, World Council of Churches,
150 route de Ferney, 1211 Geneva 2, Switzerland

No. 3 in the Gospel and Cultures series

Printed in Switzerland

Table of Contents

vii   INTRODUCTION

1   1. THE EMERGENCE OF CHRISTIANITY IN ROMANIA

23   2. ORTHODOXY AND ROMANIAN CULTURE

37   3. REGULATING THE GOSPEL AND
      CULTURE RELATIONSHIP

50   4. ROMANIAN ORTHODOXY: IMAGE AND RELEVANCE

Introduction

This short study of the interaction between gospel and culture in Romania, written from the perspective of the Orthodox Church, is also a plea for ecumenical cooperation and understanding in the country. An open ecumenical debate among all the churches in Romania about their life together and common mission is long overdue, and undertaking it would be a great service to both their own members and the country as a whole.

Romania is a country with a variety of ethnic cultures and Christian traditions.[1] Significantly, there is a close affinity between ethnic identity and confessional affiliation: nearly all the ethnic Romanians are Orthodox (only 1 per cent are Greek Catholics); the Roman Catholics and Reformed account for 5 per cent and 3.5 per cent of the population respectively, all of them ethnically Hungarian; and there are 119,000 Lutherans, all ethnically German. Overall, of the population of 22.8 million (January 1992 census), the Orthodox make up 20.3 million, or about 90 per cent.

As a result, the nexus of church-nation-politics has been and remains an element of division and tension. This surfaced again in 1993 when the Orthodox Church asked that it be recognized in the new law on religion as the "national church". The Orthodox argued for their claim both historically, as the original church of the Romanian people going back to the Roman empire, and culturally, as the source of the spiritual power which has consolidated the unity and integrity of Romania. The swift and vigorous reaction of the Lutheran and Reformed churches, combining confessionalism and ethnocentrism, suggests that neither a common national political programme nor a common ecumenical project is a realistic expectation at this point. By using culture in a strictly political way, all of the churches have politicized Christian identity.

The ecumenical picture is no brighter among the ethnic Romanian Christians themselves. The Greek

Catholics (or uniates) — who are in communion with Rome but follow a Byzantine liturgy — accuse the Orthodox of having persecuted them during the Communist era. While disregarding the dubious political origins of uniatism in Transylvania nearly 300 years ago, they are demanding on the grounds of human rights that the properties and privileges they lost after 1948 be restored to them. Rejecting the theological agreements carefully worked out in the international dialogue between the Roman Catholic and Orthodox churches, they do not accept the designation of "sister churches".

Since the end of Communist rule, tensions have also arisen between the Orthodox Church and foreign groups of "true Christians" who have come to "evangelize" the country. The Orthodox view the activities of these evangelicals as proselytism which violates the mission of the existing churches. The hostile attitude of many evangelicals towards the Orthodox is typified by a Baptist pastor in Oradea, who was quoted in a British newspaper story as saying "I would rather have an ex-Communist president than an Orthodox one". [2]

The debate on gospel and cultures cannot bypass these disputes about concepts and strategies of mission and ethnic and confessional identity. The Orthodox Church has had a long history of defending its own territory, but it is aware at least that if the language of "national church" goes beyond certain limits it becomes theological error. In the words of a Romanian bishop, "the church is and remains one, holy, catholic and apostolic. We shall never say that it is *ethnic* too. Ethnicity is not an attribute of the church but one of the conditions in which the church is localized." [3]

The study that follows keeps historical information to a minimum and concentrates on the development of the profile of the Romanian Orthodox Church as a factor creating culture and created by culture. I have sought in my comments to avoid unnecessary polemics or apologetics. I hope that, besides shedding light on some facets of the issue of gospel and culture, it will help those outside to understand the situation in Romania and encourage Christians within the country to seek ways to move beyond the unacceptable immobility created today by dramatic proselytism and ecumenical hypocrisy.

Geneva, November 1995 *Ion Bria*

NOTES

[1] For details see such standard works as David Barrett, ed., *World Christian Encyclopaedia*, New York, Oxford U.P., 1982, pp.584-88, and André Sellier and Jean Sellier, eds, *Atias des peuples d'Europe Centrale*, Paris, Editions La Découverte, 1991, pp.131-41.
[2] *The Independent* (London), 13 Dec. 1993, p.15.
[3] Metropolitan Antonie Plamadeala, "Catholicité et ethnicité", in *Deuxième Congrès de théologie orthodoxe*, Athens, 1978, p.499.

1. The Emergence of Christianity in Romania

The profile of Christianity in Romania emerged over the centuries during the course of the ethnic and cultural development of the people, a process which was inseparable from the ecclesiastical organization.[1] Within the brief compass of this booklet we cannot begin to offer an adequate survey of two thousand years of history of the Romanian people or the Romanian church. Instead, in this chapter we shall lift up some of the moments from that story which illustrate the question of the relationship between gospel and culture.

An identity of synthesis

The Romanian people are sons and daughters of the Dacians (or Getae), a people of European origins descended from the Thracians, who arrived in Moesia, north of the Danube and the Carpathian mountains, more than two thousand years before the birth of Christ. A settled population, the Dacians engaged in agriculture, viticulture, livestock and gold-mining, and were known as an heroic and brave people. To pacify them, the Roman emperor Trajan sent his armies, including soldiers from the whole empire, across the Danube. After two wars (A.D. 101-102 and 105-106), Dacia was colonized by the Roman administration, military officers and soldiers. Following the Roman occupation in 241, the Latin-speaking settlers in Dacia were incorporated into the Roman empire; and from the assimilation of native Dacians and Romans emerged a new ethnic entity: Eastern Romans known from the fourth century on as Romanians.[2]

Despite migration by various tribes — Visigoths, Huns, Slavs and Hungarians — and the invasion of Tartars in 1241-42, the evolution of the settled population in Dacia was not interrupted.[3] By the end of the ninth century, the process of ethnic formation, with a specific language and religion, had been completed, and the territorial extent of Romanian land was defined.

Language, religion, ethos and culture are woven together in this process. Due to their cultural ascendancy, the Roman settlers succeeded in imposing their popular Latin language on the indigenous Dacians, whose language was unwritten. While the Dacian linguistic heritage survives in some place names and a few common terms, the spoken Romanian language has a Latin grammar and vocabulary.

Eusebius of Caesarea (fourth century) records that the apostle Andrew preached in the regions of the Danube and the Black Sea. The population of Dacia Pontica (present-day Dobroudja) received the Christian faith at the end of the first century from missionaries coming from Greek fortresses in Asia Minor and Greece. The message was spread further throughout the territory of Trajan's Dacia, including Transylvania, by Christian soldiers and Christian colonists brought from Asia Minor and other Roman provinces, by Christian prisoners brought by the Goths and by Christian missionaries from the Roman provinces south of the Danube. There is evidence of established Christian communities among the Romanized population both south and north of the Danube from the fourth to sixth centuries.[4]

What is important here is that the ethnic formation of the Romanian people took place simultaneously with the penetration of the gospel. This is reflected in the fact that most of the Romanian Christian vocabulary is derived from the popular Latin spoken at the boundaries of the Roman empire in the early centuries. Unlike certain other peoples, there is no date to which one can point when the Romanians were formally or officially converted to Christianity as the result of a missionary campaign from outside or the decision of a political leader. The "baptism of the Romanians" in the fourth century was at the grassroots level: the *pagani*, the people of the village, became *Christiani*. So it is that Romanians appear in history as a Christian people.

Christianity was the catalyst that linked together the constitutive elements of Romanian identity.[5] The Dacians brought their religious convictions, with their spirituality of heroism and sacrifice. Their spiritual heritage of courageously facing death represented a favourable context for receiving the gospel.[6] Traces of the old Daco-Romanian spirituality (songs, stories, games, behavioural patterns with quasi-religious significance) can still be detected in Romanian culture. The Romans brought their developed language and their sense of law and justice and moral rectitude. Christianity did not destroy such realities but transcended them and synthesized them into a new identity.

Some historians have argued that the missionary penetration of Christianity into the region of Daco-Romania was part of the emperor Constantine's strategy to restore the unity of the empire through the universality of the Christian faith, its worship, institutions and symbols (especially the cross). In fact, the first local Christian communities in Romania emerged in a context of persecution. There is a list of martyrs from the third and fourth centuries from eastern and central Dacia.

Several episcopal centres are known from the early centuries, as are the names of bishops who participated in the ecumenical councils. The native church became famous through personalities like the ecumenical writer John Cassian (365-435), or the Scythian monks and theologians who proposed in 519 the well-known Christological formula "one of the Trinity suffered in the flesh", or the great historian Dionysius Exiguus who calculated, though with questionable precision, the date of the birth of Christ on which the calendar is now almost universally based.[7]

It was logical that after the barbarian invasions broke direct links with Rome the old Daco-Romanian dioceses should be integrated into the jurisdiction of the Patriarchate of Constantinople, whose territory covered the eastern part of the Roman empire. Constantine inaugurated Constantinople (formerly Byzantium) as the "new Rome" in 330. In 545 the emperor Justinian created the archdiocese of Justinian Prima, with its seat in Sardic (Sofia), which covered the territory of Dacia.

In the Romanian context, then, inculturation had a connotation and spirit quite different from the method of St Cyril and St Methodius, the "apostles to the Slavs", sent in the 9th century by the Patriarch of Constantinople to preach the gospel in Moravia and Central Europe, where they created an alphabet for the people. It is also different from the method of the much later Western missionaries who went to preach the gospel in so-called "pagan countries". In Romania Christian practices — rites of initiation, funerals, marriage, art, vestments — were introduced as part and parcel of the process of the identity-formation of the people, both cultural and social. For this reason, when the church accepted Old Slavonic as a liturgical language in the 10th through 16th centuries, the faithful continued to use their specific Latin vocabulary which they had assimilated before the baptism of the Bulgarian church in 864. Although 20 percent of the words in the ecclesiastical vocabulary are Slavonic, and this influence is obvious to this day in many church services, the particularity of the Romanian tradition is preserved especially in the language.

The emergence of an autonomous church

There is historical confirmation from the 1300s of two distinct independent lands (*voïvodats*): Wallachia or Muntenia (1330), today Muntenia, ruled by the dynasty of Bassarab, and Moldavia (1359), ruled by the dynasty of

Bogdan. Parallel to these independent political organizations autonomous churches with an episcopal structure emerged in three provinces. These were still under the jurisdiction of Constantinople, which was extended to the whole of the Balkans after the city fell to the Ottoman Turks in 1453, but the way to full autonomy was opened.

An indigenous national church cannot exist without its own language, culture and autonomous leadership. These crucial principles are interwoven in the culture of the Romanian people: cultural identity through their own language, Christian identity through ecclesiastical autonomy. Here, too, lie the roots of the "symphony" between state and church, political and ecclesiastical powers. Not only was the Christian faith accepted by the people; it also received official support in Romanian *law*. The common faith represented a unifying principle for family, community and state; and on this symphony depends the political and cultural unity of the country.

It must be acknowledged that this model is not absolute and that its ideal has not always been carried out in practice. There have regularly been times when ecclesiastical independence has taken the distorted form of autocracy. Nevertheless, cultural identity in language and ecclesiastical autonomy in the national interest constitute the panoply of Romanian Orthodoxy.

At the same time this symphony provides protection against foreign threats. From the Middle Ages on, the Romanian principalities were a frequent target of political and cultural expansion on the part of the empires surrounding them: the Ottoman, the Russian, the Austro-Hungarian. In seeking to secure the unity and independence of the nation under these circumstances, the Romanian political leaders also saw themselves as defending the Christian faith, protecting Christianity from the forces of Islam and maintaining the autonomy of the church. As time passed, the interconnections among these values became more elaborate and complex. The sense of communion of the saints, language as biblical and liturgical doxology and an emphasis on spiritual life became predominant values.

At the crossroads of cultures

Throughout the centuries, Romanians have sought to defend not only their national interests but also the wider cause of Christianity in Europe as a whole. Indeed, the country was devastated on several occasions by wars against the soldiers of the Ottoman Turkish empire. Despite victories by Stephen the Great of Moldavia (1457-1504) and other princes, Wallachia and Moldavia (known as the "Gate of Christianity") were eventually obliged to recognize the suzerainty of the Turks. But the terms of capitulation stipulated full cultural and religious autonomy,[8] and even during the period of Turkish domination, Moldavia continued the Byzantine tradition without interruption. At the crossroads between the Byzantine and Slav worlds, the Romanian principalities became the cultural centre of Orthodoxy, providing financial support and supplying theological books in Greek, Arabic, Georgian and Slavic.[9]

After the conquest of Hungary by the Turks, Transylvania became autonomous but run by the Hungarians. Romanians were tolerated, but not recognized as a nation. One way in which the Reformed ethnic Hungarians and the Roman Catholic Austrian Habsburgs sought to subject them was to find substitutes for their Orthodox faith and worship. For example, the Hungarian Prince George Racoczy (1630-48) obliged Orthodox priests in Transylvania to educate the young people according to a Calvinist catechism (printed in Romanian in 1648), to repudiate Orthodox rites such as chrismation, burial ceremonies and veneration of icons and crosses and to obey the Hungarian bishop. At the same time, the Roman Catholic Church, with the support of the Austro-Hungarian empire, continuously pressed the Romanian Orthodox to convert to Catholicism.[10] The Western powers used similar lines of argument to justify their campaign against Orthodoxy: the alleged superiority of Western Christianity, the poverty and ignorance of the Orthodox clergy, the "Oriental" mentality of the Orthodox and the servility of a nationalistic church. Thus the "union" of the Orthodox with Rome in 1700 was in effect an effort to reduce the Orthodox church to a mere "Byzantine rite" under the jurisdiction of Western Catholicism, with the promise of ecumenical and cultural emancipation for the Romanians.

There were some strong organized reactions among the Orthodox to this expansion of the Reformation and of Catholicism, not only in the Romanian provinces but also in the Ukraine and Poland. Patriarch Cyril Lukaris (1572-1638) rejected a proposal from Prince Gabriel Bethlem to convert the Romanians of Transylvania to Protestantism because, he said, they were united with Wallachia and Moldavia.[11] In 1642, following the Council of Iasi, Metropolitan Peter Moghila of Kiev published an Orthodox confession. In 1645 Varlaam of Moldavia prepared a catechism to combat Calvinistic texts that were being aimed at the Romanian Orthodox.

In this context, the church exercised vigilance not only on behalf of cultural and linguistic identity and ecclesiastical autonomy, but also on behalf of the nation as a whole. This was a particular concern in Transylvania, which had been separated from Hungary and become a principality under Turkish suzerainty in 1526. Wallachia and Moldavia were permanently in conflict with the kings of Hungary because of the Romanians living in Transylvania (55 percent of the population by 1910).

The first political unification of the three Romanian provinces took place in 1600 under Michael the Brave. This strategy was inspired by the church; in fact, all metropolitans for the Romanian Orthodox in Transylvania have been consecrated in Targoviste, capital of Muntenia.

While the cultural centre of gravity was the "Romanian lands" in the south of the Carpathians, the beginnings of Romanian literature took place in Maramures and Transylvania. The earliest ecclesiastical literature, both manuscript and printed, began to appear at the end of the 15th century. Between 1508 and 1512, Macarie, a priest in Targoviste, printed many liturgical books at the monastery of Dealu; and between 1559 and 1581 Deacon Coresi printed a series of biblical texts and commentaries, including the Psalter, in Brasov. Gradually, the Romanian language was becoming not only the language of worship but also a literary language, replacing the Slavonic officially used in church and state administration. A typical mid-16th century work is the *Teachings of Prince Neagoe Basarab to his Son Teodosie*, an original synthesis of doctrine, ethics and spirituality whose political vision is dictated by the Byzantine tradition, the formal framework within which Romanian culture developed its "Europeanism" in the next centuries.[12]

Part of the mission of the church was to translate the Bible into a language that could be understood by Romanians in all the provinces. In 1648 the first edition of the New Testament (in the Cyrillic alphabet) was printed in Alba-Iulia under the authority of Metropolitan Simeon Stefan, who wrote in the preface: "We have struggled to preserve the meaning of the Holy Spirit, for a meaningless Scripture is like a body without a soul." While scholars have differed about the motivation that lay behind this translation (some for example cite the influence of Lutheranism), the church was in any case interested in having a common and popular instrument of communication and the Romanian princes were eager to reach the cultural level of the Middle Ages. In this connection, the reign of Serban Cantacuzino (1678-88) is particularly important, because it was then that the first Bible in Romanian, the Bible of Bucharest, was printed.[13]

In view of its growing autonomy, the cultural weight provided by the translation of the Bible into Romanian and pan-Orthodox recognition marked by the transfer in 1641 of the relics of St Paraskeva from the Phanar in Constantinople to Iasi, the Romanian church was prepared to respond to the challenges of the European Renaissance. Several outstanding church leaders and scholars emerged. This was a turning point in the cultural evolution of Romania. Henceforth, the creators of culture began to see the "Byzantine" heritage more in historical terms rather than as a perennial paradigm. Local artists and scholars felt free to create their own styles. Orthodox Christianity came to be seen not simply as popular piety and irrelevant ritualism, but as a vision of the faith that transforms the human spirit and uplifts the human condition. The church offers the people not only an institutional and moral framework, but also a place where they can have a new vision of reality and of their history. At the same time, these artists and scholars were open to European and ecumenical exchange, recognizing as they did that no cultural model is absolute and that even local models will reach a point of exhaustion if they are not renewed.

A characteristic feature of the Romanian renaissance was the attempt to balance traditional values, especially Christian ethics, with openness to new discoveries in philosophy, science and culture. The sacred history in the hands of divine providence was seen as something which must be introduced into the social realities of secular history. Divine and political power are not in opposition, but must be in dialogue leading to fruitful synthesis. This view of history is also politically useful, because it helps to maintain a balance in society. The separation by the 18th-century European Enlightenment of religious from secular thought did not find fertile soil in Romania; and there was neither anti-religious philosophy nor an anti-clerical revolution.

Yet when faculties of theology were founded in Iasi and Bucharest at the end of the 19th and beginning of the 20th centuries, many of the professors had been educated in Western universities; and one can detect a certain "Latinization" and "Hellenization" of Romanian theological thought and literature. Handbooks for dogmatics and ethics, written in Russian under the influence of Latinized Greek professors and then translated into Romanian, introduced such Roman Catholic and Reformation viewpoints on Christian doctrine as the Augustinian concept of the search for God through natural meditation and contemplation (metaphysics), an intellectual understanding of the mystery of God and the incarnation and the notion of the "development of doctrine".

Nevertheless, this scholastic influence coming through the theological faculties did not change the perspective of an authentic Orthodox theology. Contact was maintained with the sources in the patristic tradition and with hesychast spirituality.

Another synthesis

Several events prepared the way for the recovery of an autonomous and autocephalous Romanian Orthodox Church between 1859 and 1925, including the national revolution of 1848, led by Nicholas Balcescu, in which the Orthodox clergy played an important role, the union of the two principalities in 1859, independence from the Turks in 1877 and recognition as a national state outside the orbit of the Austro-Hungarian empire by the European powers in 1918.

In ecclesiastical and cultural terms, autonomy and autocephaly for the church meant the liberation from several forms of captivity and a restraint on the influence of Western culture:

(1) *The hegemony of the "mother church"*. The sultan designated the patriarch of Constantinople as *ethnarch*, the leader of the "millet" of Orthodox Christians throughout the Ottoman empire. The patriarch, with the Byzantine eagle as symbol, preserves an "ecumenical" responsibility for all Christians (the Byzantine emperors conceived their power as being over the whole world, not over a particular territory or nation); he has a supranational ministry as *primus inter pares* among the equal local sister churches. Many historians believe that this opened the door to the "Hellenization" of Orthodox culture in the Balkan countries and Romania. Greek academies were set up in Bucharest and Iasi. To diminish the influence of the Greeks of the Phanar (Constantinople), the rulers of Wallachia and Moldavia confiscated the lands of the monasteries in 1863.

(2) *The claims of the "third Rome"*. From the 16th century onwards, after the fall of Constantinople, Moscow claimed to be the protector of the Orthodox Christians in the Ottoman empire. This idea nourished a Russian messianism over against the responsibility and mission of other churches.[14] For example, in 1812 Czar Alexander I annexed Bessarabia, which was stipulated as a Romanian province in the capitulations recognized by the Turks.

(3) *Freedom for the Romanian Orthodox in Transylvania*. Here Metropolitan Andrei Saguna (1846-1873) played a critical role.[15] However, in 1876 Franz-Joseph received the royal crown as emperor of Austro-Hungary incorporating Transylvania over the protests of the Romanians and Saxons. The Orthodox paid a heavy price for the union of Transylvania with Romania in 1918, in which church, nation and state were inseparable in the same struggle. Again Orthodoxy appeared as a uniting factor in Romanian history, but it was a costly unity, with many reverses, and the suffering and martyrdom continued between the two world wars, especially in the 1940s.[16]

As the church recognized, these events, in which it was directly involved, had a highly charged emotional significance. But the outcome was to give it a large national space, including Transylvania, Bessarabia and Bucovina. As a distinct and strong state in Europe, Romania became the most encompassing political force and common denominator for the whole country.

François Thual identifies the distinguishing feature of the Romanian independence struggle as its belonging to two worlds: on the one hand it is part of the Balkan world through the principalities of Moldavia and Wallachia, and is thus heir of the Byzantine empire and years of subjection to the Ottomans; on the other hand, it belongs to Central Europe through Transylvania and Bukovina, long in the orbit of Austria-Hungary. Thual underscores the importance of the decision by Bucharest in 1916 to enter the first world war on the side of the Allies:

> It seems likely today that in case of victory, each of these two empires would have seriously considered a pure and simple annexation [of Romania]. St Petersburg would have done it in the name of pan-Orthodoxy, and Vienna in the name of a territorial expansion based on the dynastic principle in the service of the spread of Roman Catholicism. Whatever might have become of such intentions, Romania in fact escaped these two imperialisms and found itself on the side of the victors, who authorized it, after long negotiations, to gather together the ensemble of Romanian lands to form a large country.[17]

In 1925, then, a church which had been present and active in the pan-Orthodox world for centuries achieved the status of an autocephalous patriarchate. To this process of integration each ecclesiastical province brought its own contribution and genius. In the ethos of *Tara Romaneasca* (Romanian land), the church remains the institution around which the life of society is organized. Its institutional visibility and prestige are thus important.

In Transylvania, which had long suffered grievously under lack of freedom, Metropolitan Nicholas Balan of Sibiu saw any mechanism for recovering confessional and ethnic unity, including ruling out uniatism, as valid and credible. In Moldavia, the pre-eminence of originality over institutional structures was more significant, as evidenced in the development of spirituality, the art of icons and painted frescoes and the veneration of saints.

The first two Romanian Orthodox patriarchs, Miron Cristea (1925-39) and Nicodim Munteanu (1939-48), tried to consolidate this integration of confessional and ethnic identity, but at once they ran up against the limitations of politics — which in principle should be guided by ethics — in ecclesiastical affairs. Moreover, the legacy of the 19th century was an amalgam of diverse values, including some philosophical trends which had appeared under the influence of Western modernism and changed the cultural context. The gap between the established church and popular Christianity, characterized by empty repetition of religious ritual, was substantial. Orthodoxy was criticized by politicians, especially Greek Catholics, and by an anti-religious propaganda which maintained that the Romanian people had never been a Christian body. Nevertheless, there were also some great personalities — writers, historians, philosophers and artists — who contributed to the effort to articulate a cultural model under Christian inspiration.

Recovering its own charisma

Amidst this confusion, a movement emerged which sought to recover the special charisma and potential communal energy of the organic link between Orthodoxy and culture, ethnos and faith. The common denominator was an *organic* conception of human history in the celebration of the great moments of life. The most creative participants in this debate was the circle of theologians and philosophers who published the review *Gandirea* ("Thought"), including Vasile Bancila, Nichifor Crainic, Nae Ionescu, Ioan Savin and Dumitru Staniloae.

For the *Gandirea* school, Orthodoxy is a constitutive element, a living stone, of Romanian culture.[18] All cultural and spiritual expressions and manifestations of the "Romanian spirit" reveal the Orthodox faith and vision: music, iconography, architecture, popular festivals, piety, social ethics, solidarity. This culture has stood and continues to stand in opposition to secularization, disintegration and nihilism. It is fundamentally optimistic, because everything is integrated into God's creation. The human being is a sample of the eternal being. Death is not a pathology or failure, but a natural part of life. Thus a funeral service becomes a celebration of the resurrection. Salvation is seen in terms not of an impersonal unification with the cosmic, but of the ecstasy of a wedding. The Romanian people approach human history with a "sense of feast".

Crainic, who was professor of mystical and ascetic theology in Bucharest, created an unprecedented intellectual ferment with his elaboration of the idea that Orthodoxy and theology are part of the Romanian cultural patrimony.[19] At the same time, by assuming that Orthodoxy belongs to the people as ethnic Romanians, he removed mission and ecumenism from the agenda of the church. The mission of the church is to defend the Orthodoxy of the place, which is a poetic and generous way of life. It is not surprising that many of the voices defending traditionalism and opposing any reforms in the church today have followed this line. For them, the only bearers of Orthodoxy in a place are those who are attached ethnically to it.

The most systematic of these authors was the philosopher Lucian Blaga, author of a *Trilogy of Culture*, which works out a complete philosophical system to explain the relationship between culture and religion. The key word in Blaga's thought is "space", which he develops in a twofold sense: how space influences human character and how the human person deals with space in religious affirmations and artistic expressions (for example, he contends that a church's confessional character is reflected in how it uses the space of its places of worship).

For Blaga, the village, with its "cosmocentrism", constitutes the stylistic matrix of Romanian culture. The style of the Romanian people is influenced by the very form of their land, which is undulatory, calm, without aggressiveness. In such a land a shepherd can sit in silent contemplation of the visual horizon, the heavens. On the one hand, his being is organically identifiable with the land; on the other hand, within the "mioritic space" (from *mioritza*, "little lamb") he is outside his nature. In his silence he realizes the monotonous existence of the supernatural Being. God is mute, like a statue, incommunicable in his mystery. The only name for God is the "Great Anonymous", the unknown Creator. [20] A personal revelation of God would be inconsistent with his absolute transcendence.

According to Blaga, God's transcendence sets a limit to the religious and metaphysical aspirations of the human being, a boundary beyond which human knowledge, sense of the supernatural and religion cannot go. Although the human religious capacity implies an ability to surpass oneself, this is subject to the unrevealed Absolute. Thus religion is only a phenomenon of culture, an heroic effort to elevate the human spirit to its highest limit, transcendent but not revealed. Religion is therefore always subjective, variable, limited to the framework and style of the human spirit. Human religious axioms are confined to negative language, and human intellectual preoccupations end up in dogma, a rational formulation of the lost borders of the Anonymous. We are condemned to live in a "dogmatic age", in which human reason can only imagine and put together its own limited revelations.[21] With the gates of revelation closed, the intellectual pressure of the religious phenomenon is a silent torture, without response from above or dialogue with God.

Crainic was among those to criticize Blaga for artificially dissociating culture from faith, inventing an isolated God without a voice to speak through the prophets, without the love to become incarnate. Blaga, he said, confused the solitude of God with isolation. Without God's revelation, the human spirit lies in the depths of depression and ignorance.

The most creative voice in this movement was Dumitru Staniloae (who wrote a book on Blaga's relation to Orthodoxy). Staniloae rejected Blaga's system as pantheistic and pseudo-theological. His own thesis was that "only supernatural revelation places natural revelation in a clear light". Blaga did not see that God's transcendence is active in the world. But Staniloae also warns against a one-sided apophatism:

> Apophatic knowledge is completed by rational knowledge of two kinds, that which proceeds by way of affirmation and that which proceeds by way of negation. It transfers both these ways of rational knowledge to a plane more in keeping with its own nature, but, when it needs to express itself — in however unsatisfactory a way — apophatic knowledge has recourse to the terms of rational knowledge in both of its aspects (affirmation and negation). One who has a rational knowledge of God often completes this with apophatic knowledge, while the one whose apophatic experience is more pronounced will have recourse to the terms of rational knowledge when giving expression to this experience. Thus when the Eastern Fathers speak of God, they pass frequently from one mode to the other.[22]

While accusing Blaga of creating a crisis of meaning, both human and Christian, in Romanian culture,

Staniloae also criticized the intellectuals for not translating Christian faith into literature, philosophy and art, leaving a vacuum which a secularized Christianity — which is the same as paganism — could fill. For Staniloae, opposing Blaga's pantheism was a covert way of combating atheism.

This controversial but fruitful dialogue among philosophers, theologians, historians, sociologists, artists, writers and politicians was brutally interrupted by the second world war:

> In their contribution to the common patrimony of Christianity, Romanian Orthodox theologians have been able to draw upon the development of a religious philosophy movement which flourished in Romania, especially after the reunification of all the Romanian provinces into one country. The dialogue between philosophy and theology has been fruitful for all religious disciplines and has resulted in the development of a unique religious approach within the traditional framework of the Romanian Orthodox Church. Indeed, it is not only the dialogue and the confrontation between philosophy and Romanian theology which has had beneficial effects for the development of Romanian culture as a whole, but also the influence of schools and trends of contemporary philosophical and theological work. Besides the influence on certain Romanian Orthodox theologians of Greek and, in modern times, Russian theology, between the two world wars the influence of Western theology, both Catholic and Protestant, became more and more evident. Little by little, as modern Romanian thought slowly developed, these influences were integrated naturally into the present theological structure during a period in which this integration could freely take place.[23]

The last work reflecting this dialogue was Staniloae's *Jesus Christ: The Restoration of Man* (1945), which stands out as a symbolic reference point at a critical moment in the history of Romanian culture.

A new political and cultural system was introduced in Romania in 1948, which began to apply the atheistic ideology to religious beliefs, traditions and practices. Separated from philosophy, theology became a lonely and vulnerable exercise. Thus a whole cultural tradition was discontinued. Today, the connection between the two has become decisive, with the church trying to revive the Christian core of Romanian culture.

Ideological eclipse and cultural conformism

After the Allies decided at Yalta in 1945 to leave Romania within the orbit of the Stalinist empire, the so-called Soviet Security Zone, the domination of Soviet imperialism in Romania had grave consequences for the church, its mission and culture. For example, as the documents and decisions from the Orthodox conference in Moscow in 1948 indicate, the Romanian church was forced to be aligned with the front of "Slavic Christianity" led by the Moscow patriarchate — and thus to be dishonest to its own history.

Naturally, the rejection of Christian faith and practice was at the heart of the programme of the Romanian Communist state. Laws on education and religious affairs adopted in 1948 severely restricted the teaching of religion, theological education, Christian mission and literature.[24] The state devised many other ways to disqualify Christian churches and institutions as well. If all these ideological pressures did not in fact create an atheistic country, they did succeed in promoting a perfidious agnostic indifference.

Since there was no intellectual justification or cultural aspiration available to endorse the Marxist ideology and the Communist system, sociologists invented the myth of a pre-Christian pagan Romanian civilization, the so-called "Romanian mythology". This attempt to rewrite and downgrade the history of the church simply disregarded the fact that there was no historical record whatsoever of these ancient mythologies and popular beliefs. Without being a popular religiosity, Christianity acquired a wide popular character in Romania and therefore a structurally Christianized culture appeared. There is no evidence of pagan mysticism.

A special campaign was organized to discredit the Orthodox, particularly the traditional styles of popular piety. In a book published by the Printing House of the Political Department, *A Church Turned in on Itself*, the author contrasted Orthodoxy's lack of modernity with the positive models of Catholicism, with its dynamic *aggiornamento* under Pope John XXIII, and Protestantism, with its openness to the secularization of former Christian societies. The Orthodox were said to be living in a different historical age, unprepared to accept modernity, captives to their "anti-Western" convictions.

Patriarch Justinian strongly opposed the implementation of the atheistic dogma that religion belongs to the private sphere. A patriotic and deeply pastoral bishop and a democratic leader who never stopped searching for more room for the church to move in society, he was well aware that the birthplace of Communism was not within Eastern Orthodoxy, that it was a Western ideology imported into Romania by force. As he understood it, stability and autonomy are the keystones of survival for the church. It is by way of an apostolate in society that priests can preserve the closeness of the church to families. And popular democracy cannot be overruled by a political party that has no national legitimacy.

With his energy Patriarch Justinian succeeded in maintaining the institutional visibility of the church. But it would be a gross oversimplification to say that the Orthodox Church, as the church of the majority, was privileged by the Communist state. Though seldom reported and largely unknown outside the country, there were humiliations and vexations of the Orthodox faithful and priests. Any critique that the Romanian Orthodox Church was complacent in the face of the Communist regime should be scrutinized with prudence and honesty. Moreover, even during the Communist period, a stream dealing with the philosophy and history of Romanian culture was active.

With the precipitous fall of Nicolae Ceausescu in December 1989 Romania burst onto the world's television screens with the image of a wasteland, people living in tents of misery and trapped in nationalistic cultural ghettos. Forty years in the Communist tunnel had blinded people and imprisoned them in their stereotypes. Under such circumstances, the task of the church is not to legitimize its past conformity to the world, but to overcome the fear of changing itself, to imagine new educational programmes, to encourage new diaconal projects.

Once again, the most unfortunate discontinuity in the history of Romanian culture was the interruption of the debate that went on between the 1920s and 1940s about the Christian image of Romanian culture, which was in fact a debate about the relevance of Orthodoxy for the nation and for Europe. And the intellectual malaise of the Communist period was aggravated by the lack of access to the research and writings of numerous outstanding emigré scholars and thinkers who now lived outside Romania, including Mircea Eliade (1907-1986) and Eugene Ionesco (1912-1994) — to mention only the two best-known.

NOTES

[1] Cf. Metropolitan Antonie Plamadeala, ed., *The Romanian Orthodox Church*, Bucharest, Biblical Institute Publishing House, 1987; Ion Bria, *Autre visage de l'Orthodoxie: Eglise de Roumanie*, Chambésy, Geneva, Editions du Centre Orthodoxe, 1981; Mircea Pacurariu, *The History of the Romanian Orthodox Church*, 3 vols, Bucharest, Editura Institutul Biblic, 1981.

[2] Constantin C. Giurescu, *The Making of the Romanian National Unitary State*, Bucharest, Meridian Publishing House, 1980, pp.11-34; Stelian Brezeanu, *Daco-Romanian Continuity*, Bucharest, Encyclopedia Publishing House, 1984, pp.11-32; Alain Ruzé, *Ces Latins des Carpathes*, Bern, Lang, 1989.

[3] The claim that the Daco-Roman native population disappeared in the 4th century to be replaced at the end of the 12th century by Romanian "shepherds" is a recent mystification of history; cf. C.C. Giurescu, "The History of Romanians in Some Recent Foreign Works", *Romania: Pages of History*, no. 1, 1976, pp.46-101.

[4] Cf. Mircea Pacurariu and A. Ciurea, "L'Historiographie de l'Eglise Roumaine", in *De la Théologie Orthodoxe Roumaine*, Bucharest, Biblical Institute Publishing House, 1974, pp.121-57; Ioan Ramureanu, "Penetration of Christianity Among Geto-Thraco-Dacians", *Romania: Pages of History*, nos 3-4, 1967, pp.54-72; Emilian Popescu, "Christianity on the Romanian Territory Until the Sixth Century", in *Romanian Orthodoxy*, Bucharest, 1992, pp.85-99.

[5] Cf. N. Iorga, "La synthèse de la pensée: le Christianisme", in *La Place des Roumains dans l'Histoire Universelle*, Bucharest, Editions Scientifiques, 1980, pp.36-42.

[6] Cf. Mircea Eliade, *De Zalmoxis à Gengis-Khan*, Paris, Payot, 1970; Ioan Petru Culian and Cicerone Poghirc, "Geto-Dacian Religion" and "Zalmoxis", in Eliade, ed., *The Encyclopedia of Religions*, New York, Macmillan, 1987, vol. 5, pp.537-40, vol. 15, p.554.

[7] Cf. Ioan Coman, "Le patrimoine de l'œcuménisme chrétien en Scythie Mineure", *Contacts*, no. 69, 1970, pp.61-85.

[8] For the texts, see Nicolae Copoiu, "Ad Hoc Assemblies in Jassy and Bucharest", *Romania*, nos 3-4, 1976, pp.251-56.

[9] See V. Candea and Constantin Simionescu, *Présences culturelles roumaines*, Bucharest, Editura Sport, 1982.

[10] See Traian Vedinas, "Between Constantinople and Rome", *Telegraful roman* (Sibiu), nos 9-10, 1991, p.4.

[11] See Aurel Jivi, "Patriarch Cyril Lukaris' Ties with Transylvanian Protestants", in *Person and Communion: Homage to Dumitru Staniloae*, Sibiu, Editura Arhiepiscopiei Ortodoxe, 1993, pp.386-96.

[12] Cf. V. Candea, "Servir d'abord le pays, puis les lettres", *Roumanie*, no. 2, 1980, p.225.

[13] Cf. Sabin Verzan, "La Bible dans la culture théologique roumaine", *Dacoromania*, no. 7, 1988, pp.115-27.

[14] For the exaltation of the myth of the "third Rome", see the *Acts of the Conference of Orthodox Churches in Moscow, 1-18 July 1948*, Moscow Patriarchate, 1950, pp.31,35,51.

[15] See Keith Hitchins, *Orthodoxy and Nationality: Andreiu Saguna and the Romanians of Transylvania*, Cambridge and London, Cambridge U.P., 1977.

[16] On this see Metropolitan N. Corneanu, *The Romanian Church in Northern Romania*, Bucharest, Orthodox Church Publishing House, 1986; M. Pacurariu, *The Policy of the Hungarian State Concerning the Romanian Church in Transylvania*, Bucharest, 1986; Valeriu Anania, *Pro Memoria: The Influence of Catholicism in Romania Between the Two World Wars*, Bucharest, 1992.

[17] François Thual, *Géopolitique et l'Orthodoxie*, Paris, Ed. Dunond, 1993, pp.61-68.

[18] Cf. Emil Pintea, ed., *Gandirea (The Thought): A Literary Anthology*, Cluj, Editura Dacia, 1992.

[19] See his *Course in Mystical Theology (1935-1936)*, ed. Teodosie Paraschiv, Iasi, Trinitas Publishing House, 1993.

[20] Lucian Blaga, *Les différentielles divines*, Paris, Librairie du Savoir, 1990, pp.25-62.

[21] Lucian Blaga, *L'Eon dogmatique: L'Age d'Homme*, Lausanne, 1988, pp.35-43.

[22] Dumitru Staniloae, *The Experience of God*, tr. and ed. Ioan Ionita and Robert Barringer, Brookline, Mass., Holy Cross Orthodox Press, 1994, p.96.

[23] Octavian Vuia, "Problems of the Relations Between the State and the Churches in the Socialist Republic of Romania", *Buna Vestire*, vol. 12, no. 1, 1974, pp.78f.

[24] Cf. "The Church in Romania", *Pro Mundi Vita Dossier*, no. 41, Brussels, 1978.

2. *Orthodoxy and Romanian Culture*

Certain distinctive features of cultural identity have been articulated through the historical development and ecclesiastical organization of Christians in Romania. In this chapter, we shall look briefly at six of these, beginning with the forces of resistance over the more than 40 years following the second world war, when the Communist government obliged the Romanian Orthodox Church to limit its proclamation of the gospel to the Sunday worship service and reduced to a minimum its opportunities to act in solidarity with society at large.

Pillars of resistance

It did not take long for the Marxist sociologists to realize that religion is not "the opiate of the people". Nevertheless, the atheist authorities were quite unwilling to accept any form of transfer of the gospel from the personal sphere to the public arena. This created a major missionary difficulty for the Orthodox Church, given its understanding of the church as communion, liturgy as the action of the people (the *laos)* and witness as "liturgy after the liturgy". [1]

As we noted in the previous chapter, Patriarch Justinian (1948-1977) did not cease to speak about the "social apostolate". [2] For him, the church could not be an institution opposed to society or the foe of the aspirations of the nation, because it is the mother of the Romanian people. Its closeness to the society grows out of its deep historical and national roots. The pastoral implications of this social apostolate mean that the ministry of the church is far wider than merely providing therapy to individuals; it extends to the transformation of society here and now. Patriarch Justinian realized that monastic discipline and the spirituality of the ordinary faithful in the parishes were central to this. Thus the promotion of monasticism was for him a way of seriously challenging the values of a secular world. [3]

Along these same lines, his successor, Patriarch Justin (1977-1986) emphasized the institutional visibility of the church. Earlier, as metropolitan of Moldavia, he had embarked on an extensive programme of restoring old monasteries and churches, some of them with well-known outside wall-paintings. Iconography is the closest thing to the liturgy, and in such a church no believer can be a simple tourist. It is a place of conversion, a meeting point with the God who makes his dwelling among human beings. Justin did not hesitate to transform these historical and artistic monuments into places for catechetical instruction as well as national education.

The present patriarch, Teoctist (1986-), shares this high esteem for places of worship, having himself founded many new parish churches and monastic establishments. The people should see and listen to the walls of the church buildings. The material, visible church is consecrated and anointed as a place where the worshipping community is in the presence of God. Within the churches, the faithful are baptized, married, reconciled. It is where they learn of the virtues of the saints, which are highly significant for the Christian life-style and culture.[4]

The effect of all these forms of pastoral ministry and resistance was to prevent a radical secularization of society despite all the restrictions imposed by the Communist government. During the Communist period, the theological schools were not much preoccupied by the confrontation between gospel and culture. The dominant culture was being expressed in literature, philosophy and art with a heavy ideological content; and the ideological underpinnings of the materialistic philosophy of Marxism persuaded the church that Marxist-Christian dialogue was out of the question. The *modus operandi* of the church was determined by its authorities, whose chief concern was to maintain a certain institutional visibility and local autonomy. Christian culture was expressed in this dialectical struggle between political conformism and ecclesiastical autonomy.

The consequences of this strategy were summed up by an ecumenical visitor from outside, Philip Potter, then general secretary of the World Council of Churches. Offering his impressions of Romania gained during an official visit there, he spoke of

> the tremendous nearness of the church to the people, expressed above all in the liturgy, when people of different ages, professions and intellectual backgrounds worship together. Worship provides the milieu for spiritual unity and cultural integration, and is a real means of extending the missionary activity of the church beyond its boundaries. Through its artistic richness and aesthetic symbolism, it becomes an icon in which the culture of the nation receives the dimension of holiness. *Cultus* and *cultura* converge in this process of transfiguration.
>
> It was for me quite clear that this nearness of the church to the people is due to the pastoral work and spiritual influence of the priests, who pay great attention to the calling of the faithful to be the priesthood of all believers.[5]

A language embodying Christian values

As we have already seen, one of the advantages Romanian culture has enjoyed from the beginning is having a Latin Christian vocabulary. During the early centuries this facilitated communication within the Roman empire and more widely in Europe.

But this linguistic development did not happen by chance. It was an historical and cultural effort which involved ecclesiastical decisions. Indeed, for several centuries during the Middle Ages the Old Slavonic language and Cyrillic alphabet were used in state administration and church services. While this may have made possible vital communication and exchange with the large family of Slavic churches south of the Danube and in the east of the country, the adoption of a foreign language for official and liturgical use also brought with it a real danger of separation between church leaders and political authorities on the one side and the ordinary faithful on the other, who continued to pray in their own language. Recognizing this, the church authorities themselves decided to reintroduce spoken and written Romanian into the liturgy and biblical texts.

From the point of view of an Orthodox theology of mission, the vernacular is critically important; indeed, it constitutes one of the important marks of an autocephalous church. Language shapes the national consciousness of a people. It was Metropolitan Dosoftei who took the initiative of introducing Romanian into the worship services with his translation of the liturgy in 1679 (printed in 1683), as well as with the poetry of his famous Psalter. The 18th-century authors of the "Transylvanian school" used philological arguments to prove the unity of origin and language of all Romanians. Among them were Bishop Inochentie Miru, Petru Mayor, whose *Elementa Linguae daco-romane sive valachiae* was published in Vienna in 1780, Gheorge Sincai, author of a *Chronicle of the Romanians,* and Samuel Micu-Klein, who printed a Romanian vocabulary of Latin origin on his *Carte de Rogacioni* (Vienna, 1799).

During the 19th century, several well-known national poets took advantage of the passionate vocabulary and lexical richness of Romanian to express religious feelings and recount parables. The life of the great poet Mihai Eminescu (1850-1889) was a continuous and intense combat with death, but against the background of a vision of the Morning Star (*Luceafarul*), symbol of eternal love and hope. For the "king of poetry", Vasile Alecsandri (1818-1890), Easter is the source of cosmic resurrection and human liberation. Alexie Mateevici (1888-1917) wrote that the Romanian language is a "treasure": not only is it the sacred tongue of the old stories told by the peasants; it is also an abundant and precious symbol: "Our tongue is to praise glory unto the heavens, to utter eternal truths in the temple and at home." The message and vision of the poetry of George Cosbuc (1866-1918) and Octavian Goga (1881-1938) was that in the midst of a cruel history, Romanians must resist in order to exist.

The list of writers and poets of Christian inspiration is a long one. Even during the Communist period, there were those who declined to submit to petty academic conventions; instead, they used poetry, theatre and novels as a counterweight to the dominant culture.

An ethos of place

The sense of kinship with the earth is dominant in Romanian culture. Using a well-known Romanian image, Valeriu Anania talks about "the weight of the soil"; and we referred in the previous chapter to Lucian Blaga's ideas about the "cosmocentrism" of the village as creator and guardian of popular culture. For Blaga the village, situated at the centre of its world, is self-sufficient. It has been able to traverse history without being troubled or displaced by the great upheavals in the world around, in effect living "outside of time". From this sense of being a world unto itself it draws "not only the power to resist apocalyptic convulsions but also and above all a determination, a vigour and an unparalleled energy for 'boycotting' history by facing it with a sovereign indifference". That has saved the Romanian people in dangerous times. Refusing to be tempted by the history which others try to impose from above, the village, "in the autonomy of its poverty and its mythical universe, has known how to keep itself intact for the epoch when it will be able to become the solid foundation of an authentic Romanian history".[6]

But there is another possible line of explanation for this attachment of the faithful to their place and their history: the idea of a "mission to the nations" or of a "church of the nations". As the recipient of *good news*, the local community appropriates the joy of this good news in its own way. The Tradition is universal, because the good news is consistent and permanent. Its saving realities are always the same. At the same time, the Tradition is local because everyone is free to assimilate it in a personal way. According to Dumitru Staniloae, a faith which springs from love creates an ethos, a style of life, which has to do not only with personal joy but also with communion with others. In their own particular way each person and each community experience the good news, which is identical and common to all.

For all Orthodox peoples religious life is very much linked with the sanctification of the universe. Since a person can only be saved in connection with the universe, everything which serves human life is consecrated: water, bread, wine. Rooms, beds, tools are sprinkled with water, icons are placed in cars, in fields and gardens, even in the stalls of the animals. One makes the sign of the cross when blessing the table and cutting the bread, at the beginning and end of the workday, when leaving home and when passing by a church. People ask for a blessing when they meet a priest or when the priest comes to their home. All of life is filled with blessing; none of it is separated from God. At the root of this is the belief "that it is through the person himself or herself that God's energies penetrate into the world. Through the human person the world, the universe, all the elements of the world are sanctified."[7]

The votive pictures painted on the narthex walls of Romanian churches portray the founder (*ctitor*), offering the church to Jesus Christ or to the Mother of God. At every commemoration, the priest remembers not only the name of the patron saint of the church, the symbol of its universality, but also the names of the founders, the proof of its historical rootage. The resulting sense of patriotism also reflects the fact that all the social and political tribulations the people have suffered have affected the situation of the church.

This sense of kinship with its own place is inevitably affected by the fragility of Romania's unity and security within Eastern Europe. The country suffered during the two world wars. It was the victim of the Hitler-Stalin alliance. It is surrounded today by a zone of potential and actual crises. Its response to destructive forces set loose by the great powers in Europe and its neighbouring countries has been a tendency to insulate and isolate itself from the world beyond. Under such circumstances, Romanian nationalism is a weighty reality for the church. In recent centuries this nationalism has served as a counterweight to the messianic imperialism Russia sought to exercise in all Orthodox countries. The reaction to the pan-Slavic and pan-Hellenic systems promoted under the influence of the European Enlightenment accentuated a retreat into the politics of national identity.

Celebrating the faith: doxology and iconography

In this attachment to the empirical place, the sense of transcendence through apophatic contemplation is not lost. Mission is the "sanctification" of the world, which is the place of epiphany where divine mystery meets human history. The mystical unification taught by the hesychast fathers and mothers in the monasteries is not absorption. In being "absorbed" in the mystery they still receive only glimpses of it; and so they need an appropriate vehicle of communication. Theology thus becomes doxology, iconography, ascesis. The nearest that the human mind can approach the ineffable mystery of God is through the art of icons. It is thus appropriate to describe an icon workshop in a monastic or ecclesiastical centre as a workshop for theology, because the notion of "theology" has a much broader sense than verbal discourse about God.

One cannot understand Romanian culture, theology and spirituality without grasping the form and content of the painted churches in Moldavia and Bukovina.[8] Churches such as those in Sucevita, Voronet, Arbore, Humor and Moldovita typify the essence of the encounter between gospel and culture: a new reality emerges, totally empirical but totally outside the world, both here and somewhere else. Culture does not simply have an interpretative role of commenting on and illustrating the gospel message to be transmitted; rather, it is a symbol unifying two realities in one. The model for gospel and culture is the incarnation, the perfect ontological synthesis.

In this respect, the paintings which represent "two churches in one" (where both the inside and outside walls of the church are painted) reveal the Christ *Pantokrator*, so central to Orthodox thought, whose cosmic rule (*basileia*) is dependent on his incarnation. The "Christ from above" which has led to so much triumphalism in church history has its counterpart in the "Christ from below" with an affectionate face, the Logos incarnate. This theology is coupled with the specific Eastern Christian practice of the "prayer of the heart", which gives the faithful direct access to the knowledge of the Logos through the divine energies.[9] It is not unusual to meet Romanian believers who are more attached to the family of God — the saints, martyrs and confessors who have been drawn by the saving presence of this "Christ from below" — than to the omnipotent *Pantokrator*. This is especially apparent in the deep liturgical devotion of the people as they assemble in the house of God. The architectural style of the churches built under Matei Brancoveanu (martyred in 1714) indicate this familiarity with God as part of culture and spirituality. It is also seen in the icon of the Last Judgment in Voronet, where the saved ones are glorified by the very glory of Christ.

The "Celestial Ladder" (Sucevita, 1584) portrays people with one foot on the ground, the outer world, another fixed in the heavens, going back and forth. The ladder is of human fabrication, fragile and leaning, but it is the only way to climb to another reality. It requires discipline physically to scale the steps of this ladder while keeping the spiritual eye fixed on the eschatological icon of Christ.

Integrity and faithfulness to tradition

Culture is not an end in itself. It should serve faithfulness to a particular tradition, which is a concretization in history of the universal and permanent divine message of good news. In a sense, any reflection on the relation between the gospel and cultures runs up against the problem of the nature of tradition. There is a dimension of permanence to the God-given revelation and saving realities of the history of salvation. This content, the good news, cannot be changed. Everyone must confess with Peter, "You are the Christ, the Son of the living God" (Matthew 16:16). In this confession the churches have a common point of reference, a basic vision of the mystery and ministry of Jesus Christ.

However, the expression of this message can take historical shape in many different ways. There is no absolute uniformity, because the church must proclaim the gospel, which means transmitting it from culture to culture, from generation to generation. There is no place for cultural formalism or theological conformism. Culture is the "stylistic matrix" (to use Blaga's term) of the good news, making it transparent and alive, able to enter the experience of the whole people. There is a paradox here between unity and diversity:

> Each people lives its faith at the same time in an original manner. Orthodoxy remains the same, it remains apostolic, it preserves all the richness of the apostolic preaching and of the life of the Christians of the time of the apostles... Each people can assimilate and express the common and universal message of Christianity with its own culture. People are different but they have common characteristics; they understand each other. There are differences but there is also a unity. There is an essence of Christianity, a permanence. Jesus is the same yesterday, today and forever. Culture is only a form; it cannot be substituted for the essence of Christianity. I remain myself in this unity, without setting up boundaries between others and myself or among the nations. We are together, but we nevertheless retain our personal or national identity. [10]

Is it an advantage or a disadvantage for a tradition to have been received and transmitted without the convulsions of Reformation and Counter-Reformation — as the Romanian Orthodox tradition was? In the first place, it is important to have within European Christianity a church which represents the original synthesis between Roman culture and Eastern Orthodoxy. Second, as we have seen, the identity of the Romanian Orthodox Church was not built up by rejecting other confessions and cultures. The conflictual movements and reforms in the history of Western Christianity did not find fertile soil in Romania, but neither did those in the Orthodox churches, such as the *raskol* movement, in which 12-15 million people rose up against the official Russian church. The Reformation principles of *sola Scriptura* and *semper reformanda*, which stimulated the missionary expansion of Protestantism, received little attention here. While Romanian missiologists and historians acknowledged the validity of these principles, the Orthodox understand the continuity and universality of Christianity in a way that does not permit using the Bible and its authority to destabilize the church or to make a critical judgment on the deposit of tradition.

In fact, the Orthodox have their own understanding and practice of mission; and there is no warrant for the charge that they are a non-missionary church simply because they have a different concept of mission from that of the Reformation churches. For the Orthodox, mission is seen as an act of sanctification ("Hallowed be your name") by Word (benediction) and sacraments (anointing). There may be some inertia and lack of evangelistic zeal associated with this attitude, but is not evangelical and ecclesiological fidelity a unifying principle for family life, for the social community of a country and finally for the universal church?

Objects of salvation: body, creation, community

A particular understanding of salvation operates in Romanian culture. The central focus is not so much on the forgiveness of sins through satisfaction or moral compensation or on the rite of absolution. Salvation is seen more in terms of exposure to divine grace, or glorification, an availability to become a "living stone", a building block in the temple. This involves several elements.

One element is the body, in the sense not only of physical corporeality, but of the entire human personality, involving the renewal of mind. This anthropological concentration is predominant in rural communities, where it takes the form of a kind of psychosomatic therapy through various rites of purification. The corporeality of the human person must be disciplined and sanctified, especially in the practices of fasting during the period of preparation for Easter and of blessing at important moments in life: birth, marriage, reconciliation, death.

Another element is a sense of epiphany, of the presence of uncreated divine energies in the empirical world. There is no autonomous natural "scientific" order in the sense of a "secular" view of the universe, since the gift of grace is not something external and supernatural, but is intricately interwoven with God's creation. This reverence for the natural world can be seen in the service of Epiphany on 6 January and in the great blessing of waters, as well as in the use of symbol of wheat and grapes — that is, bread and wine — for the body and blood of Jesus Christ.

There is also a sense of reverence for the community as it gathers — not only in the holy place of worship but also in the public marketplace, where the "other altar", the altar of the poorer brother or sister, is set up. The church recognizes both the mystery and the sociological dimension of this sacramental view. Christians can act within the visible, social structure of the church, but only in keeping with the vocation of the church to be a sign, here and now, of the kingdom of God. There are not two different systems, one for ecclesial life and another for social life. Personal ascesis and social ethics, eschatology and social teachings are interconnected.

The story of the cathedral built in Curtea de Arges in 1514, a unique florilegia of styles and colours, is relevant for the understanding of salvation here. The legend says that what the builders achieved during the working day was destroyed overnight until the body of the wife of the chief master Manole was built into the church walls. The heart of the sacrifice is not in the physical death of the woman, the burial of the human body, but in its use as a "living stone" in the edification of the church. Everyone is called to offer his or her body as a building block of Christ's body, the church.

Here the insights of Mircea Eliade are to the point. Eliade says that the attitude of Eastern European peasants, far from being a "paganization" of Christianity, was in fact a "Christianization" of the religion of their ancestors. In their seasonal festivals and religious folklore a genuine "popular theology" is at work, an "original religious creation in which eschatology and soteriology are imprinted with cosmic dimensions". Without ceasing to be the *Pantokrator*, Christ comes down to the earth to visit humble peasants, just as the supreme being did in the ancient myths. This Christ is not an "historic" figure, since the people are not interested in chronology or precise details of historical events or questions about the authenticity of historical personages. According to Eliade, this cosmic Christianity of the rural populations

> is dominated by the nostalgia for a nature sanctified by the presence of Jesus. It is a nostalgia for paradise, a desire to rediscover a nature transfigured and invulnerable, protected from the upheavals due to war, destruction and conquest. It also expresses the "ideal" of agricultural societies, continuously terrorized by warring hordes from elsewhere and exploited by different classes of more or less indigenous "masters". It is a passive revolt against the tragedy and injustice of history, in sum, against the fact that evil no longer reveals itself uniquely as an individual decision but above all as a transpersonal structure of the historical world.[11]

NOTES

[1] Cf. Ion Bria, "The Liturgy after the Liturgy", *International Review of Mission*, vol. 67, no. 265, Jan. 1978, pp.86-90; repr. in G. Limouris, ed., *Orthodox Visions of Ecumenism*, Geneva, WCC, 1994, pp.216-20.

[2] Cf. C. Pavel, "Problèmes de morale chrétienne dans les préoccupations des théologiens roumains", in *Théologie Orthodoxe Roumaine*, pp.285-399.

[3] Cf. "La Vie Monacale dans l'Eglise Roumaine", in *L'Eglise Orthodoxe Roumaine*, Bucharest, Editions du Patriarcat, 1987, pp.253-82.

[4] Cf. Metropolitan Nestor Vornicescu, *Romanian Saints and Defenders of the Ancestral Law: An Introductory Study*, Bucharest, Orthodox Church Publishing House, 1987, pp.69-101.

[5] Quoted in *Romanian Orthodox Church News* (Bucharest), no. 3, 1975, pp.89ff.
[6] Lucian Blaga, *L'Etre historique*, Paris, Librairie du Savoir, 1991, pp.232f.
[7] M.-A. Costa de Beauregard, *Dumitru Staniloae*, Paris, Editions Cerf, 1983, p.57.
[8] Cf. Vasile Dragut, *La Peinture Murale de la Moldavie, XVe-XVIe Siècle*, Bucharest, Editions Méridiane, 1983, pp.5-43.
[9] Cf. Anca Vasiliu, *La traversée de l'image: Art et Théologie dans les Eglises moldaves au XVIe siècle*, Paris, Desclée de Brouwer, 1994, p.39.
[10] M.-A. Costa de Beauregard, *op. cit.*, p.56.
[11] Mircea Eliade, *Aspects du Mythe*, Paris, Editions Gallimard, 1963, pp.209-11.

3. Regulating the Gospel and Culture Relationship

The coming together of gospel and culture in any context, including the new context in Romania, requires a certain methodological and theological "regulation". Culture is an integral part of faithfulness to a particular tradition; thus the nature of tradition is an essential part of the gospel-culture debate.

Fidelity to the tradition has two focal points: a defensive, conservative role of protecting the tradition received; and a creative, critical, missionary role of transmitting the retained tradition. Culture must help the church to remain the "guardian angel" of the gospel, not its denying angel. Under historical and political constraints, churches have often seen this fidelity to the gospel as implying a very strict traditionalism and ritualism, even to the point of rejecting other cultures and traditions. For example, the Romanians, caught between the Western Catholic and Reformation front on the one side and the Eastern Slavic world and the Islamic empire on the other, reduced their identity to an essential minimum.

The nature of tradition

Tradition is a principle of continuity, because it carries the *content* of the gospel. The Bible, which is an essential part of the deposit of tradition, cannot be used as a principle to introduce discontinuity into the tradition. Unique though the Bible's authority is in the church, the church also has its own life in Christ which is expressed beyond the written testimonies. The church has the Bible as a part of that life in Christ, and therefore it must witness to "the faith of the saints" in all times and all places. Culture must facilitate this introduction of the gospel into every new human and social context.

Tradition is a principle of "transmission" because the faith received is always a faith transmitted. The ongoing process of reception (as well as the exceptional process of reception of conciliar decisions) involves both retaining something and re-transmitting it into contemporary experience. In this movement, the church, exercising discernment, sets out the teachings of the faith — the catechetical and doctrinal formulations of the biblical revelation — in the form of narratives and parables, philosophical concepts and analysis, symbolism and contemporary language. Here there is room for creativity, imagination and reform.

But this creative and imaginative appropriation of the culture must be done with the assistance of a "guardian angel", in order to protect the mystery of God. Here lies one of the "regulations" about which this chapter speaks: the mystery of God cannot be disclosed through cultural communication, no matter how paradoxical or symbolic. Culture is not an interpretative or apologetic tool to "discover" the truth in its fullness or to understand the faith better or to make the gospel more "credible". "Inculturation" — the insertion of the gospel into a culture — means the transfiguration of that culture. For the gospel is the expression of God's capacity to change the old into the new, to make a new creation, to lift a fallen world to God's glory.

Inculturation should participate in this transformation of creation. Thus the evangelistic use of the culture is always apophatic and doxological, requiring the creation of symbols, hymns, prayers, theological vocabulary, music, iconography. Each nation must offer a place for the in-dwelling of the logos of God. The Orthodox speak about a liturgical and sacramental environment in which gospel and cultures meet together: the places of worship, the discipline of the Christian community.

Today the discipline of protecting and communicating the gospel, both within and outside the church, requires an effective language which resonates with the younger generation. Churches are always in danger of using the familiar words of the so-called sacred language — which are in fact not at all familiar to the people who attend catechetical courses or worship services.

Related to this is the problem of the analogy between symbol and reality. At one level, this has to do with the fact that although the church's traditional symbols and feasts, its calendar, its ecclesiastical rites and prayers and vestments may attract a certain religious public, they may also discourage young people from even attending worship services. At another level, it has to do with the contradictions between the official hierarchical image of the institutional church and the reality of the surrounding community, which is often defaced and deformed. For example, it is well known that in its main lines the liturgy generally follows the structure of the ceremonies of the imperial court of Byzantium. How can this type of ritual be relevant to a poor rural parish in which every economic and spiritual reality points to poverty and powerlessness? Again, Byzantine icons use blue for the king and red for the queen. But why not change the colours and style of painted images according to the reality which they seek to mediate? Surely the icon of a black African saint cannot be identical to that of a Greek saint from Mount Athos.

An authentic renewal in the visual arts, in theological vocabulary, in hymnography, in worship (including non-liturgical worship) should be encouraged throughout the church. Otherwise, the traditional concepts and canons will limit the vision of the Christian faith and dissuade the younger generation from worshipping. Does the tradition provide sufficient ground for as comprehensive as possible a renewal of the symbolism, visual art, language and worship, so that they deepen faith, aid evangelization, foster celebration in the community and enrich devotion in the home? How may the faith and the tradition be handed down to the young? Which identity should be retained by people living at the crossroads of several cultures? But it must never be forgotten that tradition lives in the process of transmission only if it does not lose its integrity.

The crisis of an equivocal "symphony"

As a consequence of the Treaty of Yalta, Romania became a satellite of the Soviet empire and a victim of the cold war politics of the great powers. The totalitarian regime installed in the country created instruments of domination and exclusion: the myth of an atheistic culture and a materialistic ideology, a view of history as the theatre of class struggle, secular axioms and values as alternatives to the gospel, submission of ecclesiastical authorities to state control. What was left of the "symphony" was only for the purposes of political propaganda.

Seduced by a certain stability and even prosperity in the church, theologians ignored sociologists who were predicting a growing secularization of the church, the end of the historical established church, the disappearance of the state-church legacy, the death of Constantinianism. One of the most devastating experiences was precisely the trap of a perverted symphony.[1]

But what should be the political stance of the church today? Both within the church and outside there is a variety of attitudes and contradictory positions. In some quarters there is a terrific nostalgia for a "Christian society" and a "Christian state" to replace the one that was ruined by the Communists. Some go so far as to call for a restoration of the monarchy. Others plead that a return to "established Christianity" is the only way to face the apocalyptic age being introduced by the "forerunners of the anti-Christ" (among them the ecumenical movement and the European Union). The church is therefore caught between, on the one hand, renascent nationalism[2] and traditionalism (nostalgia for the head of the church as ethnarch, the head of the nation) and, on the other hand, Western modernity — although it is not clear which

Western values are to be transmitted to the East other than economic liberalism and tolerance of the profit motive. On top of this comes the invasion by way of the global communications media of Western mass culture — accepted enthusiastically in some quarters as part of European values.

Liberation from intellectual conformism

In the mid-1940s, the *Gandirea* debate between Lucian Blaga and Dumitru Staniloae was interrupted. Subsequently, however, Staniloae published his landmark *Jesus Christ: The Restoration of Man* (1945); and the person of Staniloae dominated the Romanian theological scene until his death in 1993. His constant refrain was a call for a return to the creative theological tradition. "Christian tradition is never theologically exhausted," he wrote. His fame is due not only to his three-volume masterwork of dogmatic theology,[3] but to his generally imaginative thinking on basic religious issues, including his dynamic interpretation of God's revelation, which contradicted the pale and static concept of Trinity that is one of the weaknesses of most Western theology.

Staniloae made an important contribution to the methodology of contemporary Orthodox theology.[4] While stimulating interest in theological reflection, he did not invest a great deal of energy in formulating rational arguments and concepts about God, and he avoided such Western obsessions as the *analogia entis* (the idea that divine reality is a reality parallel or similar to the world), religious rationalism and spiritualism. Apologetics, he believed, inevitably does violence to human intelligence in order to demonstrate God logically; and spiritualism does violence to ethics by creating the assumption that sanctification can somehow be realized without grace. Mystical theology offers intellectual liberation, for faith does not come at the end after reason has been exhausted but is a ladder to the infinite divine reality.

We have already mentioned how "Christian civilization" in Romania was gradually supplanted during a generation of resignation and frustration. In the bitter clash between Marxist ideology and Romanian culture, values were supplanted by force, since no one was convinced of the legitimacy of the Communist system. The church was turned into a museum, liturgy into a show, aesthetics into politics, philosophy into ideology.

Now that the Communist system has passed away, the profile of the present culture remains undefined. But the analysis done so far suggests several important elements:

- The most frightening legacy of this period is the gap which has opened up between religion and ethics. Young people have lost their religious and moral bearings.

- Basic intellectual enquiry seems to have been abandoned. Some observers have spoken about a malaise of reflection, the defeat of thinking itself. There is a general lack of interest among intellectuals in religious themes.

- There is no real desire to reconstruct society, either because the reality is seen as too deformed or because the people are not convinced of any programme or committed to any engagement to change it.

Against this background, what is the role of theological reflection? Reconnection with the past is a priority for many theologians. We have already spoken about the gaps and disparities between different aspects of the same reality. The theology of *theosis* needs to be reconnected with the restoration of the beauty of human persons (consider for example the heart-rending images of the many anonymous orphaned children in Romania). The ecclesiology of koinonia needs to be reconnected with the reality of the rural communities in those villages which were treated unjustly and humiliated by the political authorities. For those scholars and artists who were forced to repeat stereotypes, the theology of icons needs to be reconnected with intellectual and artistic creativity.

Involvement in a liturgical model

What is the role of Orthodoxy in a thoroughly secularized society? What capacities does it have to navigate the present moral crisis and to avoid civil eruption and self-destruction? To use a term of Staniloae, the Romanian Orthodox Church needs to recover its potential for "Christian humanization".

The most venerated figure in Romania during the Communist period was St Calinic of Cernica, a bishop who immersed himself in the dirty and inhuman realities of the poor communities in his diocese. He knew that mystical unification with God in prayer is an act of glorification, but he also knew that "mystical theology" is not an end in itself. He discovered the Jesus Christ of history in his brothers and sisters agonizing in economic poverty and religious ignorance. Only through such an approach could the Orthodox Church succeed in being the only public institution to resist atheism.

Surprisingly, the lesson many Christians draw from this is that politics and life in society should be avoided. Inspired by certain monks and spiritual fathers, a movement has emerged calling for a return to the spirituality of the so-called "Eastern Mysticism", which promotes detachment from historical events and isolation of the people from civic affairs.

But the task of the church is precisely to help the society to shape a new economic system, to promote alternative structures that will enhance social and economic justice and lead to a genuine community of democracy, freedom and solidarity. It is true that Orthodox churches have generally declined to take a stand on concrete questions of social ethics and public life. By contrast, for over a century — and especially in the last

25 years — the Roman Catholic Church has been issuing important social encyclicals. Is the Orthodox Church ready to become more articulate on these issues and to risk taking genuine and ambitious positions — recognizing that any positive pronouncements on social issues are likely to divide the community of the faithful and make the church's voice a more lonely one? But the church is not a paternalistic institution, and the urgent requirements of the present time demand its immediate presence as a concrete and relevant force in the realities of the day.

An ecumenical ministry for a majority church

As a disciplined community, the church must be faithful to its particular tradition and the elements that make it distinct. But integrity to the tradition is not the same as fundamentalism. In facing numerous cultural changes, even the content of the tradition becomes critical. There is a lack of correspondence between the values of society and traditional culture. The frontiers between faith and culture, beliefs and mentalities, are not well defined. At the same time, ecclesiastical institutions are becoming old and fragile. This is not only a consequence of the tribulations of the Communist period. It is also a result of sociological changes, particularly the transition from rural parishes to urban communities, which has taken place without any corresponding renewal in the content and style of prayers and worship services. The greatly increased influence of the mass media — newspapers, but especially radio and television — has presented a further challenge to the integrity of the tradition.

Even before the December 1989 revolution, a member of a renewal group in the church wrote that "without a material and spiritual renewal, without a renaissance of those outdated things which are no longer kept in the light of the gospel and do not allow it to be transparent today, a living faithfulness to the tradition and a vital transmission of the faith to future generations are not possible". [5]

Being the church of the majority in the country places a significant responsibility on the Romanian Orthodox Church. In order to be faithful to the *oikoumene* it must be open to others, willing to understand others and to receive gifts from them, to pray and to learn from one another. It has a message to proclaim and a service to render to the wholeness of the wider community.

One clear example is in the area of historic ethnic tensions. Nothing can justify the permanence of these divisions. There is a crying need for Christians to speak and act in society with a common voice. New forms of Christian community and new ecclesial realities, which transcend the divisions inherited from the past, are emerging. The ideological dimension of "minority issues" has been exaggerated by the very European powers who encouraged the troublesome boundaries between states. All churches must struggle to do away with stereotypes and mutual recriminations. A part of this discipline in the case of the Orthodox will be learning to live with religious and ethnic pluralism. The price of the Great Romania of 1914-1920 was to sign in 1919 a "treaty of minorities". Since then the ethnic homogeneity of the country has been an embarrassing subject.

One challenge to common Christian witness in post-Communist Romania is the question of how to cope with the influx of conservative fundamentalist evangelists from abroad, who are taking advantage of the new religious freedom to bring a destructive form of populist proselytism. Is it possible for "sects" of all kinds, foreign missionaries and fundamentalist movements to learn how to contribute to the formation of a disciplined Christian community rather than destabilizing existing churches?

A particular form of the issue of proselytism is raised by the phenomenon of "uniatism", by which churches in some places have retained a Byzantine liturgical tradition while entering into communion with Rome. Uniatism has been rejected as a means towards the unity of the church by the international Orthodox-Roman Catholic theological dialogue, but the tensions surrounding the presence and rebirth of uniate churches from centuries past remain largely unresolved and have come to the surface in recent years in several countries of Eastern and Central Europe, including Romania.

> People are made to believe that since the liturgical rite remains the same, recognition of another ecclesial authority is merely secondary. People are tempted by the material advantages of links with the West to believe that the essence of the faith is preserved in the rite.
>
> It must be reaffirmed that Orthodoxy does not identify with a rite, be it "Byzantine" or "Eastern". Orthodoxy existed long before such rites came into being, it survived in the catacombs without priests or rites, and could continue to exist after the disappearance of the Byzantine rite.
>
> Orthodoxy is a much deeper and integral reality, from which one cannot simply detach the liturgy while rejecting the life on which it is founded. The Orthodox must deepen the existential meaning of prayer and community, just as their ancestors were forced to do when, having been abandoned by the hierarchy following the Union of Brest-Litovsk, they formed Orthodox fraternities founded on the spirit of conciliarity.[6]

Indispensable requirements

In October 1995 the Romanian Orthodox Church celebrated the 70th anniversary of its recognition by the Orthodox communion as an autocephalous patriarchate. The church cannot claim to be unaffected by the continuous but unequal tradition of these seven decades. But merely turning back to the old inherited tradition is not a viable option today. The dynamics of Christian community in the new society are totally different. Many of the concepts, orientations and institutions of the past need radical correction; and that process will require a long time and take many different forms.

If the total disappearance of what is left of religious culture is to be avoided, the church will have to give greater attention to religious education. Already it is involved in a new system of teaching religion in public schools; and new handbooks of religion are being prepared and published. Free to take responsibility in mission and education again, the church must also recognize and stimulate the teaching ministry of the laity. History offers examples enough of the experience of the people in defending the Orthodox faith. There are urgent reasons for renewing this tradition. This can take various forms: restoring the parish's sense of being a community of faith, reactivating the teaching obligations of priests and resuming the responsibility of theologians for preparing religious public opinion. The people need more clarity and understanding of the Orthodox faith if they are to give an account of the hope which is in them (1 Peter 3:15).

Perhaps the most urgent corrective to be made if the living power of the gospel is to be transmitted to a new generation is a renewed understanding of mission. Reform of the parish system cannot be postponed on the pretext of "preserving the church's identity". The present system leaves many large urban areas untouched by the gospel message. But reform should not be for the sake of renovation but to serve as an example for the renewal of society. Therefore, new Christian education in mission should be associated with the economic and political construction of a new society. What is needed is a mission in which people are called to participate in making the gospel a concrete reality in human history, to see the transforming power of grace in society, to experience the therapy of the Word of God. Without such reformulations and reforms, there are two alternatives — empty churches and parallel religious groups.

There is also a need for ecumenical analysis. The concept of the local church, based on the idea of a limited canonical territory and of a particular nation, identifiable through its culture and language, highlighted the autonomy and freedom of the people of God in a specific place. But while ecclesiastical autonomy has been a source of freedom and solidarity in the nation, it has sometimes imprisoned churches in nationalistic captivity. In our time, the difficulties churches have in coping with the rise of nationalism, ethnic divisions and civil wars in their own countries have become all too painfully evident. Therefore, analysis and strategy are required in order to make the local church, with its own particular identity and integrity, a living member and partner of the ecumenical fellowship in a country.

In Romania there is a desire to renounce the old confessional stereotypes and to remove the rigidity of the churches caught in a history of division. There are signs of common witness and ecumenical cooperation. In an age of sectarian and fundamentalistic groups, the churches cannot be completely deaf to the call to Christians to be united in Christ, here and now.

NOTES

[1] Cf. I. Bria, "Challenge to the Orthodox Ecclesiology in the New European Situation", in John Pobee, ed., *Construction of a Common European House*, Geneva, WCC, 1992, pp.81,86; "Changes in Romania", *One World*, no. 177, July 1992, pp.6f.

[2] Cf. the warning of John Taylor, in "The Future of Christianity", in John McManners, ed., *Christianity*, New York, Oxford U.P., 1992, p.656: "Patriotism is now valued more highly than ideology, and the Orthodox Church is intensely patriotic. Christianity indeed faces, ironically, the older danger of becoming in the next century uncritical and unprophetic as it is allowed to be more 'established'."

[3] Published in English under the title *Experience of God*, Brookline, Mass., Holy Cross Orthodox Press, 1994.
[4] Cf. Dan-Ilie Ciobotea, "La Théologie roumaine contemporaine", *Service Orthodoxe de Presse* (Paris), no. 27, April 1978; I. Bria, "Romanian Orthodox Theological Education: 1948 to the Present", *The Catholic World*, no. 237, 1994, pp.17-23.
[5] *Fidélité et Renouveau*, Bucharest, Editions du Patriarcat Roumain, 1989, p.6.
[6] "Dynamics of Liturgy in Mission", *International Review of Mission*, vol. 72, no. 327, July-Oct. 1993, pp.323f.

4. *Romanian Orthodoxy: Image and Relevance*

We have seen that Christianity in Romania has a long and complex history, with its sources in early apostolic times. It is thus difficult to offer a definitive and comprehensive portrait of it. Nevertheless, a distinctive cultural identity has emerged from its faithfulness to an heritage whose roots lie in both Eastern faith and spirituality and in the Roman language and ethos.[1] The transfer of Christianity into the native culture developed in various stages and according to various models. Several forms of synthesis were articulated along the way: Christian-Romanian "Latinity", a "symphony" between the native church and the national state, "Byzantium after Byzantium", resistance against powerful empires (Ottoman, Austro-Hungarian, Russian, Soviet), Orthodoxy and nationalism, a crisis of culture, dislocation of values, conformity to political standards.

In the ongoing search for a consistent vision of the mystery of Christ that is both historical and eschatological, two streams converged actively — one conservative and defensive, one creative and prophetic. Creating culture and shaped by culture, the church was aware that the gospel must transcend all cultural and historical identities. "Good news" has a permanence of content and vision. The image of Pentecost — the "church of the nations" — is vivid and enduring. However, a strong commitment to empirical realities and the historical rhythms of the people meant that the long look was not always taken. Romanian Orthodoxy has in general been open to cultural and intellectual contacts with the world beyond. It was never shut up in a cultural ghetto. Yet it was pushed during the past decades into a certain conformism of its patterns of behaviour to the political realities of the country.

Despite the immediate euphoria following the end of the Communist era, the predominant mood of Romanian Orthodoxy today is not one of utopia or jubilation. Life in society and church alike is distorted and incoherent. Nobody has yet been able to offer an adequate description of the "new reality"; and as a result the image of the country is becoming anonymous. The collapse of Communism in Romania is associated with a failure of a Christian society of reference, by analogy with the collapse centuries ago of the "Christian *oikoumene*" (the Byzantine empire). There are unresolved questions which require immediate attention: the temptation of turning the preservation of tradition into a preoccupation with national interest which excludes others, the threat of seeing culture either as the sole preserve of the established church or as an ideology in the hands of the politicians, the tendency to lift up a spirituality of *theosis* while ignoring the sin committed against the image of God in human beings.

The new theological discourse on gospel and culture which is needed must include a critical evaluation of the option of teaching Christianity as part of the history of religions, comparing it with other religions, faiths and beliefs, as well as of the position which takes traditionalism for granted, assuming that Orthodoxy is the essential core of the Romanian cultural patrimony and that the church is the defining institution for the historical continuity and spiritual unity of the country.

A fruitful point of departure for this debate could be the exceptional synthesis made by Dumitru Staniloae. Criticizing both pantheism and fatalism, he conceived God's transcendence as an active energy in the human condition and history. The trinitarian understanding of God underlies a spirituality of koinonia in which the human person is restored. Koinonia also has its repercussions in social life; thus Staniloae speaks about "Christian humanization". He had a keen appreciation for what he saw as the "bridge character" of Romanian Orthodoxy, and he constantly encouraged young intellectuals and theologians to take a more ambitious role in the reconstruction of the country and of Europe.

But the debate on gospel and cultures is not an end in itself. It must be set within the context of the church's task of mission and evangelism. For the church cannot take for granted that the Christian faith is the centre around which spiritual and social life are really organized. No one doubts that mission is an essential and permanent function of the church. But today the church must proclaim the gospel to a new religious public, within and outside its walls. This process of evangelizing takes place in a new world that is full of ambiguities, but the debate must be specific and concrete if it is to be relevant and fruitful. Equally, the debate has to be interlinked with a vision of the future, specifically, an exploration of the future of Romanian society.

What is needed is not just to challenge conformity to the old structures and stereotypes, but to think and do new things, things which have not been done and thought before. This exploration is not aimless, clueless, but confident in a deep renewal. The experience of the entire people, within and outside of the church under the Communist regime, remains a substantial and original inspiration for such renewal. What is the place of Christian faith as good news in the heart of the citizens, within the structures of society, in the ecumenical and European context? The actual understanding of Christian faith and the relevance of Orthodox spirituality are largely influenced by how they are applied and concretized in anthropology, psychology and sociology.

In the past the church looked for political archetypes, ecumenical and national. The emperor Constantine, "converted" to the Christian faith, is the patron of many churches in Romania. Prince Stephen the Great of Moldavia is recognized as a national saint. It is therefore important to see who are the figures who represent Romanian culture and society, who are the ecclesiastical leaders who have the right to speak about Orthodoxy today as good news for Romania.

Finally, at the centre of the gospel and cultures debate remains the problem of the restoration of the human person in the image of God. This is of particular significance in the Romanian context, where the image of people — men, women and children — is becoming anonymous. Lucian Blaga, as we saw, gave to the Creator the name "the Great Anonymous", a God imprisoned in his transcendental silence, hence the drama of the human search for God which cannot overcome its ontological finitude. Because of the opacity of the sinful world, there is no transfer of image from God to human being. Countering this are the painted icons, which reveal the image of God in human beings in the status of glorification. It is not only the "mioritic space" which is part of the picture of the saints, but also the divine image, which reveals the beauty of God in each saint. After decades of conformism and simple repetition, how do the people recover their own personality, that uncreated image which shapes the face of every person? Christian culture should be a formative matrix, a womb, in which every person can recover the image of God which is already hidden in him or her since baptism.

The ebb and flow of history have made of Romania, in the heart of Europe, a special case, culturally and ecclesiastically. In this context, the return of the religious has taken place amidst an unprecedented turmoil. Tyrannized until yesterday by atheistic propaganda, people today feel relentlessly pressed by the Western world to speed up the rhythm of transition and to make risky changes in the so-called patriarchal structures. But their novitiate in the new political and economic disciplines is tortuous and time-consuming. In addition to that, there is a stubborn bastion on which actual historical development has little influence. The danger is to have either a hybrid form of Christianity or a metaphysical one.

Instead of laying out foreign missionary options for the reconstruction of their country, Romanians have to be encouraged to remain consistent with their own "style" and to draw from their own resources the energy to shape a popular contemporary Orthodoxy. Virtually undiscovered yet by Europe, there is hidden treasure in the Romanian soil and soul, which bears in it wisdom, lyricism and human availability. To treat these with condescension or indifference would reveal a misperception of their potential for the future of Christian civilization in Europe.[2]

There is no reason for automatic scepticism. For there is good precedent for hopes that the stone rejected by the builders will some day prove to be the cornerstone of the building.

NOTES

[1] N. Iorga, "Between East and West: A New Romanian Synthesis", in *La Place des Roumains dans l'Histoire Universelle*, Bucharest, Editions Scientifiques, 1980, p.175; George Alexe, "Thraco-Roman Distinctiveness of Byzantine and Romanian Christianity", in *The Faith Calendar*, Detroit, 1992, pp.94-105.

[2] Cf. Georges Castellan, *Histoire des Balkans: XIVe-XXe*, Paris, Fayard, 1991.